SONGS OF THE SOUL

SONGS OF THE SOUL

One hundred Poems on Love, Loss, and Light

AMY LEE

Amy Lee
Songs of the Soul
One hundred Poems on Love, Loss, and Light

Published by Spines Publishing Platform
ISBN: 979-8-89691-598-0

CONTENTS

Part One
WHISPERS OF THE HEART (20 POEMS)

1. Timeless Reunion — 3
2. Unmatched Grace — 4
3. Yearning Across Time — 5
4. Love's Silent Spell — 6
5. Simple Wishes — 7
6. A Silent Greeting — 8
7. The Wound of Time — 9
8. Whispers Through the Night — 10
9. Yearning in Starlight — 11
10. Eternal Vow — 12
11. Graceful as a Jade Tree — 13
12. Aroma of Love — 14
13. Fleeting Glance — 15
14. A Thousand Lifetimes with You — 16
15. Side by Side — 17
16. Heartbeats of Daylight — 18
17. Lotus of Our Dreams — 19
18. Morning's Embrace — 20
19. When Friendships Fade — 21
20. Dawn's First Light — 22

Part Two
SHADOWS OF LOSS (20 POEMS)

21. Echoes of Sincerity — 25
22. Fading Dreams — 26
23. Whispered Farewell — 28
24. A Cry for Relief — 30
25. Frozen Struggles — 32
26. Secret Stream — 33
27. Together We Stroll — 34

28. Homesick Dreams — 36

29. Frozen Despair — 37

30. Bound by Fate — 38

31. The Secrets of the Sky — 39

32. Beneath the Fading Shadows — 40

33. In the Depths of Winter — 41

34. Snowflakes and Silence — 42

35. Clouds of the Forgotten — 43

36. Emptiness in Waiting — 44

37. The Weight of Silence — 45

38. In the Silence of Waiting — 46

39. In the Grip of Silence — 47

40. The Quiet Struggle — 49

Part Three
SEASONS OF CHANGE (20 POEMS)

41. The Turning of Leaves — 53

42. Winter's Quiet Wisdom — 54

43. Song of the Earth — 55

44. August's Quiet Mystery — 56

45. Whispers of Changing Seasons — 58

46. The Dawn of New Blooms — 60

47. In the Wake of Spring — 62

48. On the Edge of Growth — 63

49. When We Choose to Roam — 65

50. Fleeting Joy — 66

51. When Geese Take Flight — 67

52. Veiled Aspiration — 68

53. The Divide — 69

54. Springtime of My Dreams — 71

55. Between Light and Color — 73

56. Golden Echoes of Autumn — 74

57. The Moon's Cycle — 76

58. Revelations of the Ascent — 77

59. The Quiet Fade of Summer — 79

60. Dance of Light and Dark — 81

Part Four
RAYS OF LIGHT (20 POEMS)

61. Grace of the New Dawn	85
62. Fields of Light	86
63. Guided by Starlight	87
64. The Power of Choice	88
65. In the Quiet Light	89
66. Nothing's Lost in the Journey	90
67. Melting Frost	91
68. The Call of Distance	92
69. Bound by the Seasons	93
70. Golden Descent	94
71. Dawning Flame	95
72. Unbroken	96
73. Echo of Tomorrow	97
74. Seeds of Light	98
75. Golden Hour	99
76. Mended Glass	100
77. Rise Again	101
78. Lantern of Faith	102
79. Through Cracks	103
80. Against the Wind	104

Part Five
REFLECTIONS OF THE SOUL (20 POEMS)

81. Song of the Sour	107
82. Reflections of the Soul	108
83. Drifting Through Autumn's Echo	109
84. Moonlit Secrets	110
85. Fleeting Grace	111
86. The Power Within	112
87. The Journey to Peace	113
88. Secrets We Bear	114
89. Echoes of a Timeless Landscape	115
90. Enough for Me	116
91. A Flicker in the Lotus	117
92. The Silence Between Us	118

93. In the Light of Tomorrow 119
94. Eternal Grace 120
95. Timeless Impressions 121
96. Wings of the White Crane 122
97. The Pursuit of Joy 123
98. The Distant Path 124
99. Echoes of Divine Grace 125
100. The Snow's Solitude 126

Part One

WHISPERS OF THE HEART (20 POEMS)

Theme: Love, connection, and longing.

Introduction: Reflecting on love in its many forms—romantic, platonic, familial, and the quiet moments that fill the heart

TIMELESS REUNION

Meeting you feels like an old friend's return,
A gentle warmth, familiar and stern.
We share a smile on paths entwined,
While worlds around us fade in kind.
The stars, the moon, like dust drift by-
Yet here we stand, both you and I.

UNMATCHED GRACE

Upon our first encounter, roots of affection grew.
I only regret not meeting you earlier,
In gardens of faces, none bloom like you.
Your spirit is warm, so honest and true.
I've met many women, yet none match your grace.
With you, love finds a truly peaceful place.

YEARNING ACROSS TIME

Fighting to make two places mourn.
Longing for each other yet not close,
For whom does spring come from the heavens?
Paddling toward the blue bridge is easy to beg,
But reaching the emerald sea is hard to rush.
If only we could visit each other in Cambridge,
Facing each other, forgetting our poverty.

LOVE'S SILENT SPELL

Once we met, we knew each other well,
Our hearts entwined in a silent spell.
Before we met, peace was mine,
No longing, no aching line.
But why would I rather live in sorrow,
Face a lonely tomorrow?

SIMPLE WISHES

What I want is actually very simple.
Time is still here.
You are still here.
Happy fall

A SILENT GREETING

It's a blessing to know you,
I've prayed countless times in secret,
Hoping the dream in my heart would never fade.
If we ever meet one day,
There may be countless joys too deep for words,
But a simple smile will say it all:
"Hello"

Chapter Seven

THE WOUND OF TIME

Many years have passed, yet you're still in my wound,
I've released the world, but not the ghost of you,
The mountains stand, rivers flow, but I let them go,
One by one, I part with each, alone in the undertow.
In life's grand scheme, what truly matters, what's real?
If not the moments that bind us, and the pain we feel,
For in the end, only life and death remain, our fate to seal.

Chapter Eight

WHISPERS THROUGH THE NIGHT

I'd speak to you now, if only you were near,
In whispered tones, my heart would make it clear.
"I miss the warmth of your familiar voice,
In every silence, I find no choice."
"I'd tell you of the dreams I've yet to share,
Of fleeting thoughts that linger in the air.
Though distance parts us, my thoughts remain,
With every breath, I call your name."
So, here's my message, carried by the night,
Hoping somehow it finds you in the light.
In the space between us, my words take flight,
For you, my dear, in my heart, you're in sight.

YEARNING IN STARLIGHT

Under the midnight sky so clear,
The North Star's glow feels faint and near.
Lost in the dark with no return,
Who will heed my hearts deep yearn?
Winds whisper softly, yet none reply,
A lonely song beneath the sky.
Dreams linger where starlight cannot die.

ETERNAL VOW

I declare in this life we'll grow old side by side,
Hand in hand through spring's warmth and autumn's chill.
You say only if heaven and earth should collide,
Would we part in this life-never, if they will.

GRACEFUL AS A JADE TREE

Bound by heart and fate,
Though life is short,
Our love remains deep.
On the day we meet again in another life,
You will be a young man,
As graceful as a jade tree in the wind.
Wishing to speak of tender feelings,
longing for the red dress,
In the desolate forest and deep willow branches.
Except for the painting of the beautiful bird from that time,
Only one beautiful woman can understand the charm.

AROMA OF LOVE

The aroma of new tea fills the mouth and lips,
Complemented by the rich taste of rice cakes.
In the eyes of lovers,
There is always a beautiful woman,
Each pair lost their own passion.

FLEETING GLANCE

In the lingering scent, the bells softly chime,
Her eyes, though gentle, remain a mystery.
As she leaves, a gentle smile and a fleeting glance,
Our eyes meet in that sudden, shared moment.

A THOUSAND LIFETIMES WITH YOU

Hold my hand, and we'll embrace a thousand lifetimes,
Lost in the madness of timeless love.
With a kiss upon your eyes,
I'll share endless rebirths,
Facing every storm and hardship side by side.
In your gaze, I find my forever,
And in my kiss, a lifetime of deep affection.

SIDE BY SIDE

During your glorious moments, let me sing for you,
In sorrow, dear brother, let your heart ring true.
No roads too long, no river too wide,
Together we'll face it, side by side.
What's a bit of hardship, what's a little pain?
When you need me, I'll come through sun or rain.
Life may rise and fall, but we'll stay strong,
Our bond, through time, will carry us along.

HEARTBEATS OF DAYLIGHT

At dawn I watch the sky's soft hue,
At dusk I gaze at clouds so blue.
In every step, in every pause,
My heart, dear love, is yours because.

LOTUS OF OUR DREAMS

Let us entrust our next life to the lotus bloom,
A symbol of purity, rebirth, and eternal hope.
We will plant our dreams where still waters gently loom,
Where peace resides and time moves slow.
In this life, we'll run through each passing day,
With hearts intertwined, chasing love without delay.
Toward a love that no time, no distance, can ever sweep away.

MORNING'S EMBRACE

Good morning light, the world awakes,
With golden rays that softly break.
Each moment whispers, fresh and new,
Embrace the day; it's here for you.
Good morning, my love

Chapter Nineteen

WHEN FRIENDSHIPS FADE

If life could linger in that fleeting first embrace,
Would time still carve its lines upon each face?
The autumn wind whispers of joys now past,
Of friendships once vivid but fading fast.
Hearts that once aligned now drift apart,
Yet we name it life-a play of the human heart.
Still, in memory's glow, those moments forever start.

Chapter Twenty

DAWN'S FIRST LIGHT

There is a beauty, she like dawn's first light,
From that moment onward, she haunts my day and night.
Short apart stirs a longing deep and wild,
Yearning so fiercely leaves reason beguiled.
Play my music, each note a quiet plea,
Hoping my heart's virtue draws her nearer to me.

Part Two

SHADOWS OF LOSS (20 POEMS)

Theme: Grief, separation, and the ache of what has been lost.

Introduction: Exploring the tender pain of goodbyes, the emptiness of longing, and the process of healing.

ECHOES OF SINCERITY

Profound love is not like fleeting clouds,
It lingers, unspoken, in the silence of the sky.
A pine earring stone adorns your head, like the Morning Star,
But if sincerity is betrayed, it fades, a quiet sigh.
In its stillness, it whispers no more, only the echo of a goodbye.

FADING DREAMS

Tears swallowed in silence, too late for regret,
Memories etched in faces I cannot forget.
Eyes once bright, now heavy with sorrow,
A heart's deep ache no canvas can borrow.
Words of farewell, too sharp and too clear,
At midnight, our dreams disappear.
You've woken early, from love's fleeting gleam,
While I am still lost in yesterday's dream.
Again and again, the tears softly fall,
As night rain taps on the cold eaves' wall.
The wind sighs low, and the bell softly rings,
Echoes of love in the sorrow it brings.

Chapter Twenty-Three

WHISPERED FAREWELL

The tender moment when you bow your head,
Like a spring willow retreating from the breeze.
A soft "take care," a whisper in the air,
With those words, a sweetness full of sorrow.
The silence between us speaks so much more,
A bittersweet farewell we cannot ignore.
In your gaze, I find both love and longing.

Chapter Twenty-Four

A CRY FOR RELIEF

My heart is heavy, burdened with grief,
Seeking a hand to bring some relief.
Words fall like raindrops, lost in the breeze,
Searching for comfort, but finding no ease.
The silence echoes louder each day,
A cry for help, but none seem to stay.
Who will share this pain I cannot release?

Chapter Twenty-Five

FROZEN STRUGGLES

Troubles gather, swirling in my heart,
Rising, then sinking, never to part.
The night stretches long, with no end in sight,
A quiet struggle through the endless night.
The wind whispers snowflakes take flight,
The moon shatters the ice with its fragile light.
I'm still

SECRET STREAM

Tears fall, a secret stream,
Eyes once bright now lose their gleams.
The spring breeze stirs, yet all feels wrong,
A fleeting shadow of a hopeful song.
In endless sighs, the heart does stray,
Dreams of joy seem far away.

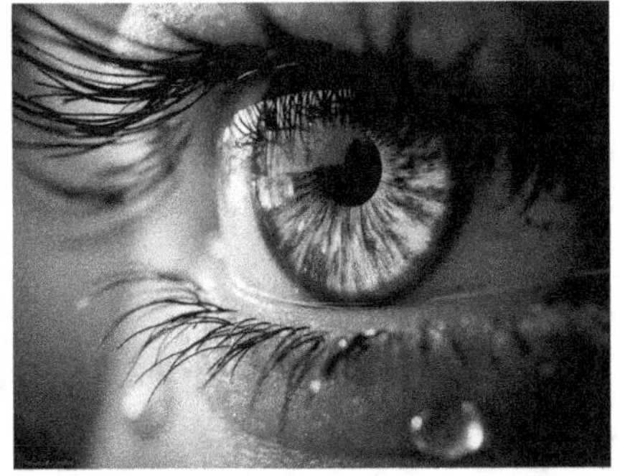

TOGETHER WE STROLL

In my heart, you are the brightest star,
Guiding me close, no matter how far.
Your smile, a spark that lights the night,
In your arms, all feels pure and right.
With every breath, you fill my soul,
In your love, I find myself whole.
Forever bound, together we stroll.

HOMESICK DREAMS

When I was young, the moon was longing for home,
It was at the edge of the sky, and I was on Earth below.
When I grew up, my grandmother became my yearning,
She was on that side, and I was on this side, still learning.
Now my Candy is my homesickness so sweet,
She laughed at me everywhere, every day,
Yet I live in a dream, incomplete.

FROZEN DESPAIR

A heart full of sorrow, yet none to share,
Turning away, I see despair.
Even tears seem worthless now,
A broken soul, but no one cares.
The snow is cold, the blooms are dim,
The moonlight chills, but colder is my heart within.

Chapter Thirty

BOUND BY FATE

Are we fated to meet, you and I?
Like a river's source and end, so distant yet tied,
Forever apart though bound in flow,
Yearning, yet unable to know.
Or is it that fate keeps us apart?
Time leaving sorrow, heavy on the heart,
Lingering grief that knows no end,
A lifetime of ache I cannot mend.

THE SECRETS OF THE SKY

Longing and yearning, we gaze from afar,
Yet never able to touch, nor to be nearby.
The sky holds our secrets, its vastness so deep,
A distance between us, as endless as years.
Who embraces springtime on this earth embrace?
Is it for you, or for the world to chase?

Chapter Thirty-Two

BENEATH THE FADING SHADOWS

In shadows cast by fading light,
I wander through the echoes of our night.
Every glance recalls a silent pain,
As distance grows, like an endless rain.
The water stretches wide, a void so deep,
Where whispers of lost moments softly weep.
Alone I search for solace in my dreams,
But darkness swallows hope, or so it seems.

IN THE DEPTHS OF WINTER

In the depths of winter,
when snow falls softly like a sigh,
The air is sharp, and the world is a quiet, frozen sky.
Yet by the stove, where warmth and wine embrace,
Your smile, like sunshine, makes the cold feel divine.
A fleeting moment, but it stirs the air.

SNOWFLAKES AND SILENCE

Raise my cup, alone I drink,
Snowflakes swirl as my thoughts sink,
Another year fades, lost in the night,
In the stillness, time takes its flight.

CLOUDS OF THE FORGOTTEN

The bright moon laughs at my lonely state,
Wasting the tender springtime heart.
Fearing to speak of the past,
Where can I find the clouds of my dreams?

Chapter Thirty-Six

EMPTINESS IN WAITING

Do you know why you're lonely, shedding tears alone?
Do you still wait for comfort, for someone to atone?
How laughable it seems, this sorrow you bear–
Turning to find only emptiness there.

THE WEIGHT OF SILENCE

How long does it take to write a single word to you?
Only I know. I met you; you met me.
But my courage to look back is smaller than dust.
I walk forward into the wind, feeling the cold against my
　　face-
As if it's the shadow of you, silent and still.

IN THE SILENCE OF WAITING

Tonight's stars aren't the same as those of last night,
I linger alone in the damp and the chill till the light.
The wind murmurs secrets only silence can hear—
And I wonder, who am I waiting for here?
Is she? still her!

IN THE GRIP OF SILENCE

The world unravels in a misty haze,
Where paths are lost in a foggy maze.
Spring's sorrow wraps me in its quiet grip,
And my heart trembles with each fleeting slip.
In silent hours, I search for peace,
But all my dreams just fade and cease.
Still, the ache lingers, refusing release.

Chapter Forty

THE QUIET STRUGGLE

I often smile, but I'm not happy.
The winds of this world blow too hard, taking all the
gentleness away.
They say that if you cry into your pillow, you'll drift into
dreams of the sea.
How is it that I can't even gift myself any joy?

Part Three

SEASONS OF CHANGE (20 POEMS)

Theme: Transformation, growth, and the cyclical nature of life.

Introduction: Life's rhythm mirrors the seasons—change is inevitable, beautiful, and often bittersweet.

Chapter Forty-One

THE TURNING OF LEAVES

The autumn breeze whispers soft and low,
A song of change where shadows grow.
Leaves ablaze with fiery hue,
Drift from branches, bidding adieu.
In their descent, a story unfolds,
Of endings and beginnings, a tale retold.
In falling leaves, life's promise is true.

WINTER'S QUIET WISDOM

The frost settles deep, the world grows still,
A quiet pause upon the hill.
The trees stand bare, their branches stark,
But under the ice, life leaves its mark.
Though winter's grip seems cold and tight,
A seed of growth stirs out of sight.
For every end, a new dawn will rise,
Transformation waits beneath winter skies.

SONG OF THE EARTH

The mountains and rivers grow brighter,
With grass and trees singing in delight.
Green seedlings spread across the land,
A peaceful joy we understand.
Voices rise in grateful song,
To bless the days both fair and long.

Chapter Forty-Four

AUGUST'S QUIET MYSTERY

Nobody speaks of August's silent grace,
As summer fades and autumn's not in place.
Fields and melons on the earth,
Make me ponder how dreams and life enthrall.
In the quiet shift from warmth to chill,
I search for threads that bind yet can't distill.
In fleeting moments, mysteries align,
But understanding slips through time.

Chapter Forty-Five

WHISPERS OF CHANGING SEASONS

The seasons change, forever in motion,
In spring, you left behind petals in devotion.
Graceful, you parted, your smile bittersweet,
Leaving autumn's sighs, quiet and discreet.
Now the clouds of fall have drifted and gone,
As winter's gray stretches on and on.
Can you withstand the cold wind's lonely song?

Chapter Forty-Six

THE DAWN OF NEW BLOOMS

The breeze whispers goodbye to the fading spring,
As the rivers stir, and birds take wing.
Snowflakes dance, ushering in the new bloom,
While petals murmur secrets in soft perfume.
The sky turns from dark to golden light,
As day rises, chasing away the night.
Nature awakens in colors pure and bright.

Chapter Forty-Seven

IN THE WAKE OF SPRING

When you come, spring will arrive,
With blooming flowers, the world comes alive.
The air grows warm, the sky so blue,
When you stay, spring stays too.
In every moment, I feel it anew.

ON THE EDGE OF GROWTH

For countless years, I wandered far and wide,
Home is always distant, like a fading tide.
Upon this peak, I stand, alone, and still,
The world below me is quiet, vast, and chilly.
Rain falls softly, its whispers fading slow,
In this solemn place, where no echoes go.
I wonder how long before my heart can grow.

WHEN WE CHOOSE TO ROAM

No road is longer than a single step,
No mountain looms above the heart's true depth.
With courage as our compass, we can roam,
For every journey starts when we choose to roam.

FLEETING JOY

A single thought stains the forest green,
A single thought turns autumn's sheen.
One thought ushers in the frost's embrace,
One thought deepens the season's grace.
The silence of leaves as they drift away,
The brilliance of kumquats at the close of day.
With a brush dipped in autumn's glow,
I paint a fleeting joy in the evening's flow.

Chapter Fifty-One

WHEN GEESE TAKE FLIGHT

In autumn's glow, the colors gleam,
Oranges and yellows weave a dream.
A long wind whispers, geese take flight,
Beneath tall buildings, hearts feel light.
Trees wear their robes of crimson and gold,
Mountains bask in the sunlight's fold.
Chrysanthemums in hair, a joyous sight,
As the autumn wind brings change to event night.

VEILED ASPIRATION

The mountain rises high, reaching the skies,
This beauty is distant, veiled by clouded sights.
Yearning thoughts, like flowers, softly speaking,
My heart races swift, its pace unique.

THE DIVIDE

In life, half is luck, and half is fate.
Youth slip away, a shadowed gate.
Half fierce, half free, I drift and sway,
One part in rapture, one in dismay.
Half my tyrant, half my peace,
A heart split in fire and sea's release.

SPRINGTIME OF MY DREAMS

You stepped from the springtime of my dreams,
Where blossoms danced in sunlight's streams.
The flowers still bloom, though seasons wane,
Each petal whispers your name in vain.
The past may linger, but hope takes flight,
In memories we hold, our hearts unite.
Together, we weave love's endless light.

BETWEEN LIGHT AND COLOR

You have no reason to feel frustrated,
For you are autumn, still in bloom.
No need to stand with pride,
For you are spring, in full costume.
Lift your gaze, and you will see,
Autumn's colors pale in spring's light.
Yet spring's glow is not as strong,
As autumn's hues, bold in the night.

GOLDEN ECHOES OF AUTUMN

It is autumn, early autumn,
The wind should still be gentle.
The sun continues to smile that smile,
Glistening with gold and silver,
Boasting of its truly scarce
Most luxurious mornings and evenings!
Here and there, in this early autumn

THE MOON'S CYCLE

This month drifts silent, soft, unseen,
Next month's promise sharp and keen.
The full moon glows with gentle light,
It wanes and waxes through the night,
A timeless dance, serene, pristine.

REVELATIONS OF THE ASCENT

You can deceive others, but not yourself.
As spring unfolds, youth shed its mystery.
The upward path is rugged and steep,
Where dreams falter and promise sleep.
It's hard to preserve the first spark of romance,
Yet some find joy while others know sorrow's stance.
Each mountain crossed reveals a true self.

THE QUIET FADE OF SUMMER

In the yellow pond, white ducks glide,
Sorghum stalks stretch, reaching wide.
How can my heart find peace on this path,
As August's call stirs a lingering wrath?
The sky, fresh from rain, glows with light,
Yet dreams remain out of sight,
As summer fades into the night.

Chapter Sixty

DANCE OF LIGHT AND DARK

Sometimes rain falls, yet the heart sings brightly,
A sunlit smile beneath a cloudy night.
Other times, warmth wraps the world in gold,
But inside, shadows whisper untold tales.
In every contrast, our truths come alive,
A dance of light and dark, where feelings thrive.

Part Four

RAYS OF LIGHT (20 POEMS)

Theme: Hope, resilience, and finding strength amidst adversity.

Introduction: Even in the darkest moments, light can find its way in, guiding us toward hope and new beginnings.

GRACE OF THE NEW DAWN

Love the morning sunlight's warm embrace,
Awakening the longing for a new chase.
Yesterday's sorrows fade like night,
God grants me strength, a fresh delight. Each morning,
Your mercies come anew, Grace like rain, steady and true.

Chapter Sixty-Two

FIELDS OF LIGHT

If you're not feeling happy enough,
Don't furrow your brow too deeply.
Life is inherently short.
So why cultivate bitterness?
Open the dusty doors and windows,
Let the sunshine and rain spread to every corner.
Step out into the open fields of life,
Let the wind smooth your forehead.
Vastness can dilute sorrow,
And dark hues can cover light ones.

Chapter Sixty-Three

GUIDED BY STARLIGHT

With passion in my heart, I seek my dream,
A vision of peace, a steady gleam.
Through winding paths and rugged trails,
I'll journey on where hope prevails.
Oh, the starry night so bright and vast,
Its silver glows my shadow casts.
The starlight guides, the wind sings low,
With peace as my goal, I'll onward go.

THE POWER OF CHOICE

Don't let one noise bring you low,
For struggles mark the path we go.
Even the sun, in its dazzling light,
May be cloaked by clouds in flight.
Your talents wait, a hidden treasure,
Until you claim them at your leisure.
Only by choice can you obscure
A bright future, a path secure.

IN THE QUIET LIGHT

A life needs places to pause,
Each stop lit softly in the fog.
Even if no one is there
To shield me from the wind,
May the light still guide those who journey on.

NOTHING'S LOST IN THE JOURNEY

Let's not give away what we hold so dear,
For treasures given fade year by year.
What's easy to acquire is seldom held tight,
True worth is found in struggles and fights.
Let them seek and learn the cost,
In the journey's value, nothing's lost.

MELTING FROST

Winter bites with its icy breath,
A world cloaked in stillness, a hint of death.
Yet her love shines bright, a radiant sun,
Melting the frost till the cold is undone.
In her embrace, warmth, and spring become one.

Chapter Sixty-Eight

THE CALL OF DISTANCE

Shouting is the burst of silence,
Silence, a voiceless call.
If the distance beckons,
I will walk toward it all.
With feet worn and torn,
There's no mountain I won't scale.

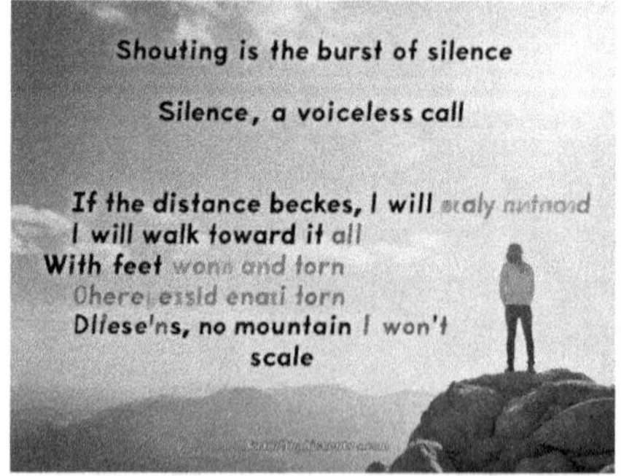

BOUND BY THE SEASONS

Fleeting thought stirs leaves to dance,
The chill of autumn whispers through the air.
Each tear, a warmth in memories' trance,
Old stories linger, wrapped in silent care.
Though flowers fall and rivers softly weave,
I stand in wonder yet cannot leave.

GOLDEN DESCENT

Every tree wears autumn's crown,
As golden leaves drift softly down.
Mountains glow in twilight's grace,
Nature's canvas, a warm embrace.

DAWNING FLAME

Beneath the ashes of despair,
A spark ignites, fragile but rare.
It whispers, rise, though faint it seems,
Kindling life in shattered dreams.

UNBROKEN

Storms may bend but not define,
Roots that hold, hearts entwine.
Though shadows fall and skies collapse,
The soul persists, the thread adapts.

ECHO OF TOMORROW

A gentle voice calls from afar,
Through every wound, through every scar.
It says, "Keep walking, don't let go,
Beyond this night, new rivers flow."

SEEDS OF LIGHT

Even in soil cold and grim,
Hope plants itself on edges thin.
In time, the bud will split the stone,
And bloom where no life was known.

GOLDEN HOUR

The in-between of dusk and dawn,
Where light renews though night has drawn.
A reminder there's a turning tide,
Even shadows serve to guide.

MENDED GLASS

Shattered shards in trembling hands,
Refuse the weight of fate's demands.
Piece by piece, a work of art-
Resilience sewn in every part.

RISE AGAIN

Falling is not where stories close,
Each end contains the seed that grows.
A phoenix soars from what is burned,
Every scar a lesson learned.

LANTERN OF FAITH

In trembling palms, a fragile glow,
A lantern lit to face the snow.
It flickers, wavers, but does not die-
A beacon against a merciless sky.

Chapter Seventy-Nine

THROUGH CRACKS

The world may crumble, edges fray,
Yet light will find its secret way.
Through cracks it seeps, and shadows dance,
Giving broken dreams another chance.

AGAINST THE WIND

The gale is fierce, the night unkind,
Yet forward steps a steady mind.
No force too strong to halt the fight,
When hope's the banner held in sight.

REFLECTIONS OF THE SOUL (20 POEMS)

Theme: Introspection, inner peace, and spiritual musings.

Introduction: Quiet moments of self-awareness, finding beauty within, and connecting to something greater.

Chapter Eighty-One

SONG OF THE SOUR

Bitter winds howl through the cracks of my soul,
A tang of regret fills the empty bowl.
Lemons of memory squeezed dry of their light,
Leave shadows to linger in the folds of the night.
Yet even in sourness, a song still takes wing,
For pain has its verses, and loss has its sting.
The sour is the sweetness that life could not bring.

REFLECTIONS OF THE SOUL

In moments still, I sit and breathe,
A quiet space where I believe.
In silence, truth is softly found,
A peace that speaks without a sound.
The world may rush, but here within,
I seek the light that sparks my skin.
Beneath the noise, I find my way,
A boundless grace that guides my day.

Chapter Eighty-Three

DRIFTING THROUGH AUTUMN'S ECHO

The scent of autumn lingers, then fades from the mat; alone,
I drift upon my small boat, beneath the sky.
Who sends the messages from the clouds, so soft and high?
As wild geese return, moonlight bathes the western air.
Flowers fall with grace, and waters move with care;
In solitude, I reflect on two places where sorrows grow.
This love, unyielding, cannot be contained or freed—
It travels from my brow to my heart, forever in need.

Chapter Eighty-Four

MOONLIT SECRETS

Only the moonlight has seen everything in this world,
Its silver gaze unraveling stories long unfurled.
Only the moonlight understands the fate of you and me,
Whispering secrets carried across the endless sea.
Only the moonlight can fill my entire bag,
A quiet treasure for journeys when spirits sag.
Only the moonlight, steadfast and glowing,
Guides to my steps where dreams are flowing.

Chapter Eighty-Five

FLEETING GRACE

The snow is like plum blossoms, soft and white,
Falling in silence, a dance in the night.
Plum blossoms are like snow, their petals so pure,
A fleeting beauty, delicate and sure.
In their likeness and difference, wonder is found,
Both fleeting and timeless, where grace does abound.

THE POWER WITHIN

In the quest to meet the world's call,
We forget the power within us all.
Chasing praise, we lose our true light,
Neglecting the heart, dimming its brightness.
The soul withers when we forget to care,
Dreams fade when we leave them bare.
Self-love awakens, restoring what's rare.

THE JOURNEY TO PEACE

A familiar yet distant face, joy or sorrow unknown,
Drenched in memories, I drifted alone.
I've tasted love in bloom and decay,
And found peace only by letting go.
Through mountains and rivers,
I seek a calm release,
A face without regret, a heart at peace.

SECRETS WE BEAR

How many secrets must we bear alone,
To walk life's path and call it our own?
In lands where heaven's light falls close and bright,
Yet hearts sink heavy, shadows dim their flight.

ECHOES OF A TIMELESS LANDSCAPE

A symphony flows from wind to wind.
Sunlight casts in many directions.
You and I are figures in a painting,
Flowers bloom to a deep, rich red,
Green duckweed covers the lake,
Birds sing as treetops weave delicate branches,
While white clouds carry us through layers of sky.

Chapter Ninety

ENOUGH FOR ME

I long for fog, wind, and a setting sun.
If the apple is ripe and smoke rises,
A bird rests on a treetop as the leaves start to sing.
In these moments, the world feels perfect, despite its flaws.
The rustling leaves carry a hopeful melody,
As evening settles with simple peace.
This is enough to love this broken world.

A FLICKER IN THE LOTUS

If my heart were a lotus flower,
It would hold a lit candle in its center.
Though its light is but sliver,
I want it to shine with pride.
Drifting with the waves of fate,
It's a fleeting guest in the universe, a beautiful dream.

THE SILENCE BETWEEN US

I understood you from your eyes
You figured me out from my words
Restraint is a character trait
Boldness is a virtue
Don't tell me
That only the eyes
Are the true reflection of the soul
Without language in solitude
All we harvest is silent...

IN THE LIGHT OF TOMORROW

In this fleeting life, I've known such grace,
Moments of joy in your warm embrace.
When youth return in a future bright,
Will our paths cross again, in the light?

ETERNAL GRACE

Oh, Creator of all that lives and breathes,
In verdant fields and ancient trees,
In every heart that beats and sings,
Your love and grace, eternal springs.
Guide me, Lord, with a steadfast hand,
In every step, in every land,
To walk with faith, to trust and see,
Your boundless love, for eternity.
So here I stand, in awe and praise,
My voice uplifted, all my days,
To worship You, forevermore,
My God, my Light, my endless shore.

Chapter Ninety-Five

TIMELESS IMPRESSIONS

Tiny black words, washed away with ease,
Yet the heart's inner images never cease.
No matter how hard one tries to erase,
They linger, vivid, in their timeless place.

WINGS OF THE WHITE CRANE

White crane in the sky, so serene and free,
Lend me your wings for a moment, I plea.
Guide me through clouds where dreams take flight,
With your grace, let me soar through the night.
Carry my heart to where hope still gleams,
Above the world, in the land of dreams.
Through your flight, I'll find what life means.

Chapter Ninety-Seven

THE PURSUIT OF JOY

A future goal ignites our hearts with light,
Like a moth drawn to the flame's embrace,
Ready to be captured by the fire's might.
In every step, your purpose finds its trace,
As your tassel swirls in graceful flight,
In love's embrace, we can't define the taste,
But once we choose, there's no turning back—
If you must lose, lose to the chase,
If you must wed, let joy be the pact.

Chapter Ninety-Eight

THE DISTANT PATH

I do not care if I succeed.

I have chosen a distant path ahead.

I only care to brave the wind and rain.

I do not care if I win love.

I am devoted to the rose and to sincerity.

I do not fear cold winds behind me.

My focus is on the horizon, leaving only my silhouette.

As long as I love life, everything will unfold as it should.

Chapter Ninety-Nine

ECHOES OF DIVINE GRACE

O Creator of galaxies and atoms, Infinite and intimate.
I lift my voice to You in awe and praise.
You know my name, Your number every hair upon my head
In the depths of my soul, you reside,
A light that never dams, a love that never fades.
You are Alpha and Omega, Beginning and End, Eternal One.
Your wisdom surpasses all understanding,
Your mercy flows endlessly like a river.
For You have seen my deepest sorrows,
And turned them into joy.
You have heard my whispered prayers,
And answered with a resounding yes

THE SNOW'S SOLITUDE

Love the snow, not like the crowd,
Who praises its dance? So soft and unbowed.
Its winter bloom, serene and bright,
Adorned in beauty, pure and white.
Love the snow for what it bears,
A spirit born of lofty airs.
It falls from heaven, proud and free,
Untouched by earthly vanity.
Unlike the flowers bound to the land,
Their roots to flattery firmly stand.
The snow is pure, with grace untamed,
Unsoiled by praise, by none proclaimed.